Black

Black

The brilliance of a noncolor

Alain Badiou

Translated by Susan Spitzer

polity

First published in French as *Le noir. Éclats d'une non-couleur*, © Autrement, Paris, 2015
This English edition © Polity Press, 2017

Polity Press
65 Bridge Street
Cambridge CB2 1UR, UK

Polity Press
350 Main Street
Malden, MA 02148, USA

ISBN-13: 978-1-5095-1207-2
ISBN-13: 978-1-5095-1208-9 (pb)

A catalogue record for this book is available from the British Library.

Library of Congress Cataloging-in-Publication Data

Names: Badiou, Alain, author.
Title: Black : the brilliance of a non-color / Alain Badiou.
Other titles: Noir. English
Description: English edition. | Malden, MA : Polity Press, 2016. | Includes bibliographical references.
Identifiers: LCCN 2016020612| ISBN 9781509512072 (hardback : alk. paper) | ISBN 9781509512089 (pbk. : alk. paper)
Subjects: LCSH: Black. | Color--Psychological aspects. | Color--Social aspects. | Symbolism of colors.
Classification: LCC BF789.C7 B3313 2016 | DDC 152.14/5--dc23 LC record available at https://lccn.loc.gov/2016020612

Typeset in 12.5 on 15 pt Adobe Garamond by
Servis Filmsetting Ltd, Stockport, Cheshire
Printed and bound in the UK by CPI Group (UK) Ltd, Croydon, CR0 4YY

For further information on Polity, visit our website:
politybooks.com

Contents

Translator's note

In *Le Noir*, the original French edition of this book, the adjective *noir* and the noun *le noir* are, as might be expected, ubiquitous. But their cumulative impact on readers of this translation will no doubt be somewhat attenuated owing to the simple fact that English uses not just one but a variety of terms to convey their meanings. Thus, the adjective is often rendered as "dark" rather than "black." Similarly, the noun offers the translator a range of choices, depending on the context: "black," "the black," "blackness," "black person," "darkness," "the dark," etc. Alain Badiou is well aware of the pitfalls of the translation of *noir/le noir*. He claimed, for example, in his 1988–89 seminar on Beckett and Mallarmé, that the phrase "in the dark" in Beckett's prose poem *Company* was much weaker than its counterpart *dans le noir* in the author's own translation of that work into French. The French language, Badiou concluded, "radicalized" Beckett's thought. In this book, he again highlights, as it were, the "black" vs. "dark" problem from an ontological point of view when he comments on the English translations of "*trou noir*" – "black hole" – and "*matière noire*" – "dark matter" – in the chapter entitled "The metaphorical black of the Cosmos."

Childhood and youth

Military black

I was a senior airman – one of my many incarnations – back in the day. The 3rd Air Region band. Dark blue uniform, cap, white gaiters, piccolo, my fingers and lips accustomed to the shrill high notes of our old warhorse, the chorus of *La Marseillaise*, which was played on every occasion. Nothing black, in other words, except the winter nights. The regulation stipulated that at 9 pm we had to put out the coal stove – aha! a touch of black in the décor (let's make a note of that), with the bucket full of coal and the pervasive, sticky coal dust everywhere – which gave off heavy smoke amid our neatly aligned beds.

Our very lives were at stake. If the regulation

wasn't enforced, said the staff sergeant, a first-rate trombonist, the carbon monoxide would quickly kill a sleeping soldier, even if he was a member of the band. The black coal couldn't have cared less that, without us, the 3rd Air Region would be deprived, and for a long time to come, of the chorus of *La Marseillaise*. And who was responsible for making sure that the above-mentioned regulation was enforced? The senior airman, who, by reason of his rank, was appointed Barracks Chief, with no resistance possible. Thus, coaxing, bargaining, coercing, bringing extra blankets, browbeating the trumpeters, cracking down on the clarinetists, being easy on the flutists and tough on the drummers, I ruled over the coming of the freezing dark. Putting out the stove, putting out the lights, ensuring that, no matter what, the bitter cold and the vast night descended on all these young men bundled up like sausages in countless layers of scratchy military blankets – that was my duty, my mission.

So, when I'd overcome the last resistances and we were all freezing together in the musical, patriotic night, my friend the oboist, in a soft yet strong voice, would start singing (or might have started singing, later on) the famous

Johnny Hallyday song "Noir c'est noir, il n'y a plus d'espoir"[1] [Black is black, there's no hope anymore], like one of those melancholy lullabies he was a great connoisseur of, or like a hymn of resignation. And we'd all join in, the way we did with the lullabies, keeping the evil powers of the night and the cold at bay this way, since singing of black despair is some consolation for having to endure it.

[1] Black Is Black," originally released in 1966 by the Spanish band Los Bravos, was covered as "Noir c'est noir" the same year by rocker Johnny Hallyday in France, where it went on to become a hit single.

The Stroke of Midnight

I was eight years old, don't worry, well before I was a senior airman in the 3rd Air Region band. But I was already interested in controlling the dark. As a matter of fact, I made up a somewhat suspicious game called "The Stroke of Midnight." To play the game, our group had to have at least five or six kids in it, and above all it had to be co-ed – which was certainly not the case with the hopelessly single-sex band whose nocturnal ruler I later became. However dark they all may be, the various "strokes of midnight," the comings of the night, may not necessarily be alike. "Black is black," sure, but there are secret and exquisite differences between them. And that's why, in the end, there's always a little hope.

Six was the ideal number of players, and the ideal ideal, which was rarely attained, was for there to be three girls and three boys. The game only began after dark. In addition, it was essential that parents of any sort, at any rate the ones who lived in the apartment we were getting together in, be out of the way: at the movies, at some late dinner, at one of the tense political meetings of the time. This was in 1945 – can you believe?! What dark times those parents were from! And what a lot of soon-to-be-dashed hopes were attached to the end of that darkness! But regardless of whether they were in the film-lovers' dark of screen images or absorbed in the unlikely clearing of our country's darkness, the important thing for us, the players of "The Stroke of Midnight," was that the parents be out of the picture. What stringent requirements! I learned from this that darkness is only exquisite when it is, if not outright prohibited, then at least temporarily free from the forces of prohibition. Let's make a distinction between official darkness, which is the regulated cessation of active daytime, and unofficial darkness, artificially induced darkness, the darkness mobilized against daytime so that action at once restricted[2] and infinite might emerge in it.

When we played "The Stroke of Midnight" at my place (at my parents', in other words, but they were out of the way), two of us, preferably a girl and a boy, would go out of the big "children's room" (meaning my brother's and my bedroom) and wait in the hallway, "with no peeking allowed" – the fundamental prohibition! Yes, the real dark, the dark of all the "Stroke of Midnight" games, freed you from the constraints of the day, but it imposed an order of its own. Surrounding the sacred dark there had to be false daylight – or even fake darkness – so that you could take part in the adventure of *entering the true dark*.

With the two selected players standing outside in the hallway and the bedroom door shut tight, the other players would make the room pitch black. There had to be complete and utter darkness. We would track down any light coming from between the slats of the shutters, from the space under the door, from any vague

---

[2] "Restricted action" is the title of an 1897 essay by Mallarmé describing the limits and focus of poetry's action. Badiou has referred to it in a number of his works.

reflections, from the keyhole. We wouldn't allow the slightest gap in the dense darkness we'd created, which was like a sort of empty promise – with no sign of light, even if nearly imperceptible – of a different world from that of daytime, parents, school, family meals. Once this point of indistinction had been reached, we would all hide, clumsily – it's hard not being able to see anything, being completely "in the dark" – underneath the beds, on top of the desks, in a closet, or in a corner.

On the order of the leader, namely, myself (as the aristocrat who invented the game, I was never one of the players who had to wait outside; I was the ruler of the dark), all the hidden-in-the-dark players would shout in unison in as creepy a voice as possible: "The stroke of midnight! The stroke of midnight!" And then the two selected players, the two outcasts from the dark, would come back into the room, close the door and grope around in the dark to try to find the hiders. Said hiders were required to defend themselves, even before they were found: they had the right to throw things at the seekers, to trip them, pull their hair, lift up their skirts, and so on. But if the seekers caught one of the hiders firmly, then, according to the rules, they could – and this was the most important point of this whole ceremonial Constitution of the dark – do "whatever they wanted" to him or her.

Once someone was captured, everything became focused on this infinite manifestation of the "whatever they wanted." In the dark, strange things happened that the spectators, blinded by the darkness they had themselves created, could only guess at, anticipate, expect, or hope for. The two selected players would give a few whispered hints in the form of orders: "Take that off!" "Not like that!" "Do it to both of us!" And on and on it would go . . . Nobody knew when the light would come back on in the bedroom, when the dark would give way, as it reasonably should.

Nevertheless, the two selected players would eventually say: "Lights on!" And the rules were that we were then to see nothing out of the ordinary: the selected players and their captive, male or female, or both, would seem to have returned unchanged from the other world, and their faces would appear as neutral as they were calm. That was the rule, too: there could be no daytime trace of the dark. The dark was where the act took place, where being so close to it thrilled the players who couldn't see, but what had taken place had to be forgotten in daytime.

In this game, the dark connoted *jouissance,* admittedly bordering on uncertainty and fear, though ultimately triumphant, no doubt, but only so long as, every single time, when the dark gave way to light, nothing had taken place except the dark of the unseen place.

The black dog in the dark

I was ten years and a few months old. Back then, summer vacation began on July 14, the French national holiday. On the 15th, my parents would send me off to a tiny little village in the Pyrenees, in a valley where, alongside short meadows strewn with menacing rocks, the bright glint of a stream could be seen between the trees. This time, alas, it wasn't about parents being out of the way so that we could enjoy playing "The Stroke of Midnight" once more. Rather, it was my parents who, eager to have me out of the way on some trip they were taking to Italy to rekindle their romance, dropped me off, miles from anything, at the home of a fine, upstanding lady. A former schoolteacher, a widow who'd become the village's only shopkeeper, she provided all kinds of goods and services in her home, which had become a real treasure trove: a restaurant, a grocery store, a dry goods store, a little drugstore, a hardware store, jerry cans of gasoline, inner tubes, flypaper, and a few rooms to let, in which I never saw anyone but myself. Vivacious and bossy, she loved me, that's for sure, as the child she had never had. So she fondly believed that she had to be tough on me.

In particular, every evening at dusk she would send me out to get milk from a farm high up in the hills. Lugging a big milk can, I would get there by a steep rugged path, with tall hedges on either side that became high scary walls at night. I'd walk along uneasily in the dark, lonely night. I was gripped by fear: I knew that at a certain moment a big dog with a black coat and shining eyes was going to start following me, silently, and would try to bite my legs. I would try to vary my pace, to anticipate the spot where the dog would emerge from the hedges, to flick a cigarette lighter . . . But almost every evening, the dog would foil my maneuvers, and, though he didn't always bite me, I knew that, as he was often so close to me, he still wanted to, and he sometimes succeeded.

Walking along the dark path had become a daily source of anxiety that I nevertheless didn't dare tell the fine, upstanding lady about, for fear she'd make fun of me. I kept to myself this genuine, nightmare-laden fear of the dark, most likely stemming from the distant past, from some nocturnal abandonment of the baby I'd once been, whose hopeless despair was revived by the sudden appearance of a night-dog.

In this case, darkness symbolized fear, anxiety, monsters and ghosts.

The inkwell

Ink was black, in inkwells and bottles, in the past. It would get all over your fingers because it would run and flow relentlessly. This inevitable messiness was the flip side of writing. I always felt caught between two kinds of black: that of the dirty and dirtying substance and that of the signs that miraculously emerged from it through the magic of wayward fountain pens, which, when dipped too deep in the inkwell, had a strong tendency to cover the paper with what used to be called "inkblots."

Oh, the miracle of a clear and possibly elegant sentence emerging from the sticky ink and wending its way between the blots! It is the black of meaning wrung from the black of matter.

School, through its most compulsory basics, reading and writing, thus taught us the rudiments of the dialectic that I'll comment on many times in this book, the formidable dialectic of black and white. Think about the exams, compositions, quizzes, extra homework, all those pitfalls of learning. Don't you say, when you've failed miserably, that you handed in a "*blank* [i.e., white] paper"? And, conversely, if you've been seized by inspiration, can't you proudly proclaim that you've "*blackened* six pages"? At school – to quote Mallarmé, the great poet of black-on-white – here, "the empty paper which its whiteness defends" happens to be the enemy that must be defeated, while the black signs, overcoming that sterile whiteness, are the key to victory. A fragile victory, moreover: it mustn't be undermined by too many horrible inkblots. For then the whiteness will triumph: because its original virginity has been stained, we will ultimately yearn and long for it.

Even if, on the wings of inspiration, you've blackened many a page, you'll be informed that the amorphous black of the inkblots, destroying the graceful curve of your letters, has resulted in a "sloppy" paper. "Not bad," the fearsome teacher will write – in red – "but too many inkblots and smudges tarnish [*noircissent*] your good intentions."

In the child's torments over pens, pen cases, recalcitrant ink, paper, intense inspiration and accidental inkblots, the insistence of the Letter[3] and the dirtiness of its medium, the underlying complexity of writing already begins to appear: there must only be black on white, but not too much of it! With just the right amount of it, when it's controlled and shapely, it's the occasion of salvation. But when there's too much of it, when it's out of control and shapeless, it comes close to Hell.

Isn't the most profound education the one that was afforded me at my childhood elementary school, the one that divides the ink sharply between thought become Letter and drive turned into splotches and blots? How will those who begin with the darkish gray on the palish gray of computer screens manage? Without the slightest inkblot? Won't they think that thought is just another variation of formlessness, that the intel-

---

[3] Cf. Jacques Lacan, "The Insistence of the Letter in the Unconscious, or Reason since Freud."

lect is just a thin additional coat of gray over the gray of drive, and drive a mere stripping of the gray of the intellect?

Everything in the world is the result of a creative and careful dosing of black as it is projected onto the formidable invariability of white. Anyone who hasn't experienced this, and sooner rather than later, will never learn anything.

Chalk and markers

It was a revolution, yes, it really was: slowly but surely, black markers replaced white chalk, while the whiteboard replaced the blackboard. No one yet knows what the pedagogical, psychological, sociological, indeed political, and even – we're at the pinnacle of modern hierarchies here – economic effects of this reversal of a centuries-old (What am I saying! Maybe even a thousand-year-old, if not longer!) relationship are. Such a fundamental institutional order can't be overturned with impunity.

Only a few short decades ago, the teacher [*le* or *la professeur*] (in those prehistoric times no one used the very feminist form *professeurE*) was still someone dressed in sober attire who would stand on a formal podium, and, with their back to the class, wield an unmanageable rag, gradually becoming covered, as the proof went on, in a light coating of chalk dust. As for the student, to be "sent to the board" and quizzed relentlessly was to be covered in ridicule, for their crooked handwriting, and in the same disgusting chalk dust, which often rendered the sorry spectacle even sorrier by making them sneeze their head off every time they shook out the rag.

And what about now? *La professeure*, the female teacher (the male teacher is an endangered species), like a female orchestra conductor, wields the long black marker on an ostensibly immaculate white board, while the student being quizzed makes the marker screech painfully, tries to wipe away their illegible scribblings with a dirty, ineffectual sponge, and, the black marker having run out of ink, covers over their dismal, poorly erased mistakes by the exotic means of some extra red, blue, green, or even yellow markers.

Who would dare to say that an inversion of that magnitude, accompanied by the use of god-awful colors, has no effect on the educational transmission, via the board, of the syllables of an alexandrine or of the roots of a quadratic equation? In geometry, a circle can be changed into a line by inversion. So just imagine if the black circle on the whiteboard becomes not just a line but a *yellow* line. Then, in addition to the strict and archaic opposition between the blackboard and the white chalk, or between the circle and the line, modern schoolchildren will be able to say that they've seen, seen with their own two eyes, that in geometry an inversion changes black into yellow.

Let's face it, the black marker and its colorful variants on a whiteboard is to white chalk on a blackboard what fast food is to authentic cuisine: since the black-and-white dish is tasteless now, all that's left is a bland of green-and-yellow spices.

Confusions

Isn't it in drawing class that we are most violently confronted with the pitfalls of black? And also with the traps set for it by the neighboring colors (if it's possible, which I doubt, to "neighbor on" true black)?

My Cartesian mind has always protested against the name "black pencil" for what clearly has a gray, literally leaden appearance and makes gray or possibly dark gray marks, but no more than that, just as talking about "black clouds" is nothing but inexcusable poetic license: no cloud is truly black. Put some real coal next to it, or the sheen of an authentic top hat, or even a simple, natural crow, and you'll see! Just because dark gray constantly claims to be black doesn't mean we have to go along with it. Even modern computer printers maintain the confusion. The basic ink, the one that's not Magenta, or Yellow, or Cyan (what a lexicon!), is designated as Black, but its result on the paper, as it suddenly emerges from the mouth of the printer like someone fleeing a catastrophe, is evaluated – a simple return to reason – in terms of "grayscale levels."

This confusion between black and gray was one of the reasons I used to give everyone who asked me why I was so bad at drawing. I admit that there were plenty of other reasons. I admit I could go on and on. Whatever the reasons were, drawing a clear glass vase with a black pencil that scribbled in gray was something I could never manage to do.

My tenth-grade drawing teacher's passion, as it happened, was to make us draw endless vases, jugs, flasks, cups, and bottles, all with just the so-called black pencil. It was all about acquiring a "sense of volume," he said. But how could that be done with black alone? Doesn't relief imply that you work with shades of gray, the way the basic printer does, which, it's true, didn't exist when I was in tenth grade, and especially the 3D printer, which existed even less, if possible? Black,

I thought, was unsuitable for volume. At any rate, my drawings were ultimately flat black, the murky night in which all vases, flattened and distorted, get muddled up [*envasés*]. No water, no ambrosia, could ever be held in my all-too-black vessels.

My teacher's sarcastic remarks about my inability to conjure the belly of the vases from my black pencil went so far as to compare me to Picasso, with his decomposed volumes, angular flatness, cardboard bottles, and harsh black where you'd expect subtle gray. And, trust me, this comparison wasn't flattering to me. Because as soon as my teacher's thinking had brought him into the vicinity of the word "Picasso," he would get this snide, disapproving look on his face and mutter: "Picasso! Picasso! He's a smartass!"

Goaded by the sarcasm and anxious not to become a "smartass" like Picasso, I made some vague progress, positioning myself between gray and black so as to produce some unclassifiable shapes, half-vase, half-cloud, but shapes nonetheless.

And this earned me the following comment for Drawing on my end-of-the-year report card: "Alain Badiou: Some glimmers of light in the dark."

Well, how about that!

Early sexuality

In the olden days of my adolescence, no one knew much about sex. It was really, as has long been said only about female sexuality, or sometimes about the unconscious itself, the "dark continent."

And in fact, our sources on the subject were composed of shady magazines that we used to buy under the counter, with titles like *Frissons* [Thrills] or *Extases* [Ecstasies] – or even, more precisely and under the growing influence of English, *Sexy Girls*. These materials, which we would peruse in avid little groups, as far away as possible from the various parental or school authorities, provided us primarily with photos of women in various states of undress, in black-and-white of course.

Nowadays, it takes no more than a click on a keyboard to reveal to young kids, in full color and motion, a staggering quantity of nude or quasi-nude men and women thrashing around in accordance with commercial categories as rigid as the ones in supermarkets, from ordinary fellatio to the most exotic combinations, all of them with English names like "blow job," "whipped ass," "cuckold sex," or "MMF," which should be understood as a trio of two males and a female, not two Mobsters and a Felon. I should also mention "lezdom," which has nothing to do with a home invasion of lizards [*invasion de Lézards à Domicile*] but with Lesbian Dominatrixes, just as "threesome," in this context, doesn't mean the Troika that oversees Greece's wayward finances on behalf of noble Europe but any sex act involving three people, not just two, let alone only one. All of this leaves nothing in the dark, absolutely nothing – except maybe love, which it's harder to reduce to the status of a consumer product on the computer supplies shelf.

In the past, where these kinds of plastic-wrapped sex materials were concerned, there was a shortage, not a surplus. A crucial added complication stemmed from the fact that the censorship of the day was draconian when it came to three prohibitions. First, it allowed shady magazines to circulate but strictly provided that they did not appear where newspapers and magazines were sold legally. Thus, getting your hands on these delectable photos of more or less nude "sexy girls" required ingenuity, diligence, and not a little cash. Second, nudity was accepted in the photos but couldn't be extended to the points and issues the censors regarded as having a strategic value. For example, you were allowed to see breasts but not nipples. In no case were you allowed to see a woman's pubic or underarm hair. Naturally, the male sex organ – erect, it goes without saying, but even unaroused, or flaccid – was forever banned.

From these prohibitions flowed a number of very important consequences, all of which had to do with the color black.

First of all, the priority accorded by our magazines to female nudes seen from behind. Indeed, from that angle, nothing was banned, since there were neither nipples nor hair. Nor a penis, except in the very unlikely case of some unnatural combination. So this left in the dark the most inscrutable enigma, the female genitalia, which was the desperately desired answer to the question "What do girls have under their skirts?" That the answer, ultimately, was that they have precisely nothing was itself rendered impossible by the prevalence of the backside, which doubtless offered a few variations on what we knew about boys' backsides, but none that was essential. Thus, the censorship unwittingly made sodomy seem self-evident, because it left the key issue of the dark continent in the dark.

Second of all, when the magazines deigned to include a female nude seen from the front, and even if it happened that the young lady had no panties on, the censors required that where the furry triangle, necessarily black in a black-and-white photo, was, there had to be a blurring of said triangle. In place of the real black there was a whitish or pale gray area, a cloud of sorts, which, as though attracted to women's crotches, lingered over them, unfortunately, just when the photo was being taken. Thus, the whiteness negated the blackness and, with it, any access, once again, to the enigma of women. And this whiteness was especially strange in that it also floated into the beautiful nudes' armpits, like a soft wad of absorbent cotton. This exacerbated our confusion: what was this mystery hidden under women's arms?

It should also be noted that the absence of panties was rare, and so, page after page, the pubic triangle's blackness made itself fervently desired, until eventually it was shown only to the extent that it was suppressed. I remember the epic tale, in one of the magazines I read in a dark corner of the gym – an appropriate place! – of the hesitations of a woman who was gradually won over by love and so allowed the man to undress her, with photos accompanying the story. The style of the story was spare but lofty, such that when the woman gave up her last garments, the text read – the phrase is engraved in my memory – "her panties, that final defense of struggling modesty." But after the collapse of that defense came the whitish cloud of censorship over the blackness of her genitalia, which made it impossible to understand why it should have taken so much time and pussyfooting around just to reveal a new and definitive obstacle to our thirst for knowledge.

Nowadays, when shaving the pubic area completely has become common practice, the real absence of black, by restoring the genitals to their childlike appearance, leaves the enigma of sexual difference intact. Thus, from the whitened black of the 1950s to the shaved black of today, photos of the female nude have always set up a disappointment whereby female sexuality persists in being at the heart of a dark continent.

It's only when black is veiled in white, when it's missing from where it's supposed to be, that we desire its real. Black is, par excellence, the colorless color of fetishes.

The dialectics of black

Dialectical ambiguities

Scientists confirm it: black is not a color. It does not appear as such in the spectral analysis of light. To be sure, our visual system, our beloved eyes, do not see everything, not by a long shot! Our rainbow, that miraculous arch connecting rain and sun, sets out its shimmering, sparkling palette, from red to violet. It includes neither the very low frequency of infrared nor the very high frequency of ultraviolet. But there is nothing to suggest that black is the extreme of everything below red, nor that it is way up above ultraviolet. No! Black is the absence of light and therefore the absence of any wavelength in the analysis of what black negates.

But is absence a negation? There's no light,

there's no color, but does that mean that light is negated? That black has successfully fought off the colors? Isn't it an overestimation of black's power to think it capable of negating anything whatsoever? No, black negates neither light nor the colors. It is their pure absence. Black is passive negation; it merely indicates the absence of its extreme opposite, light.

But isn't that glorious light the pure whiteness of which black is merely the absence? Don't we have to return to the fatal couple of black and white?

So let's watch out for the pitfalls of white. Scientists confirm it: white is only a complex, constantly changing result, an evanescent combination. Because what is the whiteness of light if not, as prisms and rainbows show, the combined, confused sum of all possible colors?

Black is the absence of color, while white is the impure mixture of all the colors. But "to have seen it all" [*en voir de toutes les couleurs*, literally, "to have seen it in every color"] is a sensibly negative expression. It reminds us that it's not good to see only white, that phantom of the sum of all the colors dissolved in their Whole.

Black is the Void of the colors, white is their

All. But the fundamental complicity between them stems from the fact that with both of them – as in the black-and-white photos of the naked women that I spoke about – the color of the real fails to be attained. Reduced, like the writing of black signs on white paper, to an austere symbolic function, the black–white opposition, despite its dialectical authority, conceals the fact that both terms equally negate what makes up the multifaceted flavor of the visible universe.

Conventional wisdom implores us "not to always see the black side of everything." But would it be any better to always see the white side of everything?

What is missing from both snow and night is the rainbow.

This explains why it's self-evident, for us decrepit Westerners, that black is the color of death and mourning, while the Chinese, who are more ancient than we are and will be around longer, think it's white.

Beware! Macbeth's black witches and Hans Christian Andersen's Snow Queen belong to the same world.

Black souls

Let's take the phrase "the darkness of the human soul" and analyze it closely. Methodically and completely.

1. We always assume that not much is known about this fatal darkness. But then some horrendous incident or another brings it back to mind and reveals its implacable, secret existence to us. "What darkness the human soul is capable of!" we moan whenever we hear about some unspeakable betrayal, some crime we shudder at having only narrowly escaped, some terrible atrocity that sends countless shivers down our spines, without our being able to give ourselves an out by pretending that the facts were falsified! The blackness of

the soul is never a simple presence; it's always a revelation.

2. Black, here, is more opposed to purity than to white. When, in Act 4 of Racine's *Phaedra*, Theseus falsely accuses Hippolytus of being Phaedra's lover, what does the young man say in his own defense? He very naturally invokes blackness to characterize the scandalous accusation and to oppose the serenity of truth to it: "In just resentment of so black a lie / I might well let the truth be known ..."[4] He takes it for granted that black, which is already the color of treacherous, murderous, incestuous souls, is by extension the color, or the sinister absence of color, of groundless accusations, of rampant slander. And what does he counter this blackness with? With this: "The daylight is not purer than my heart."[5] We of course note an allusion to light, constitutive of day, as distinct from the shady allure of the dark night. But the attribute of "heart," another name for the soul, the attribute opposed to the blackness of the lie, is purity.

[4] Jean Racine, *Phaedra*, tr. Richard Wilbur (New York: Harcourt, 1987), 73.

[5] Ibid., 74

We're already leaving the realm of colors or indeed of the dialectic of day and night, of light and dark, of white and black: if the blackness of the soul is opposed to its purity, it is because *black connotes impurity.*

3. And so it is indirectly, through negation of the negation, that white connotes purity, including in its most physical form, namely, female virginity, whether it's a question of the veil of girls taking their first communion or the sumptuous attire of brides. We shouldn't be fooled by the whiteness of these materials: it is secondary to the blackness of which it is the conspicuous negation. Like Christ refusing to bow down to Satan, the pure soul clad in white says: *Vade retro, Satanas!* Which is proof of the primacy of black Satan, whom purity, clothed in white as battle armor, struggles to fight.

4. It is striking that whiteness, in this case, actually symbolizes that form of weak negation that is ignorance. Young girls and brides are pure only insofar as they don't know what darkness the soul is capable of. As in the popular proverb, and the story of Little Red Riding Hood as well, they haven't yet "seen the

wolf."[6] Made innocently white by society, they are only so because, for a short time yet, they know nothing about the dark Phallus.

5. In short, black is the color of the soul only to the extent that it has been revealed to us by some unforeseen event. White is merely the phantom of ignorance. All knowledge is knowledge of black, which happens by surprise.

6. And Satan calls the shots. What do we call him again? The Prince of Darkness, isn't it? Thus, all the white in the world is invoked only to keep the Dark Prince at bay, to however small an extent.

---

[6] "*Avoir vu le loup*" ("to have seen the wolf") means to have lost one's virginity.

Soulages' ultrablack

Which of our contemporaries can provide better evidence of the dialectic I've been talking about here than Pierre Soulages, whose entire body of work has been devoted for many years to what he calls "ultrablack," a monumental exploration of the purely pictorial resources of black?

It is of great interest to me that Soulages regards this black – and painting as a whole – as unrelated to both pictorial imitation and description in language. Indeed, in 1984 he wrote: "From very early on, I practiced a kind of painting that dispensed with images and that I never considered as a language (in the sense that language conveys meaning). Neither images nor language."

A good approach when it comes to the dialectics based on black is to inscribe them neither in images (what could black, the notable absence of light, be the imitation or copy of anyway?) nor in language (what could black, as black without white, its writing medium, be the verbal articulation or the separable inscription of?).

But then, what is black, as emblematic of Soulages' painting? Contrary to the purity of daylight – the daylight of Hippolytus's heart – might it be the symbol of a sacred devoid of any God? Soulages lends himself to such an interpretation when he says that the Chauvet Cave's artists, 30,000 years ago, or Lascaux's artists, 15,000 years ago, ventured deep into the pitch-blackness of the caves to paint a luminous conviction in black on the walls. So it should be said that black, as the noncolor of painting, is not the opposite of light but the basis for *a light other than light.*

Soulages has stated on many occasions that there is a pictorial triangle made up of: the "thing" that is the work (since the latter is neither image nor language, it's the thing that asserts nothing but itself); the person who created it (the painter); and the person who looks at it (the viewer). The thing is a mediation between the artist's partly blind quest and the viewer's partly aware quest. I think this relationship between blindness and awareness, which implies three terms (two subjects and a thing), explains why the best "thing" possible is ultimately for the artist to show the viewer the infinite luminosity, the new luminosity, latent in black. In this sense, Soulages' ultrablack is indeed the pure pictorial affirmation of what painting is capable of.

The space created for the viewer standing in front of Soulages' immense black polyptychs is such that the viewer's movements, the way he or she walks around, make the various ultralight lights and the noncolor colors created by the black change from moment to moment. Thus, the pictorial triangle becomes: the painter's varied traversal of the black; the thing exhibited as an infinite synthesis of the lights in the black; and the viewer's constantly shifting gaze teasing out part of this infinity.

At bottom, the solitary, dense black of any painting by Soulages suggests that it could go on, that the painting's limits, and even its immensity, are only one aspect of its own limitlessness. It is in this sense that black is the basis for ultrablack.

The painter-Subject and the viewer-Subject share the incompleteness to which only black can attest. The former cannot claim that the activity from which the work derives is definitely finished, nor can the latter claim to be done with what his or her gaze can discover. As in the prose works of Beckett, who, you might say, invented the ultrablack of writing, the artist's ethics has only one imperative: Go on. Keep searching, beyond the black, for the ultrablack of the black, and so on.

With Soulages, the solemn unity of the paintings, held together by the vast expanse of the inflections of black alone, is but the arena, or one could almost say the fiction, of an infinitely complex, open network of relationships that the viewer's gaze gradually reveals. And in the end, these relationships transcend the black unity that contains them because the gaze, combined with the displacement of the body in space, discovers that they are, quite simply, infinite. And all the more infinite, I'd say, since they are not restrained, or constrained, by an image, by a story, by any meaning imposed on them, or even by a single interpretation. The serene, monumental unity of ultrablack, which is truly like a realm beyond the sea[7] then, is the painterly landscape of a world without borders and of an infinite potential of perspectives and meanings.

The perfect imperfection of black, revealed by Soulages' painting, lies in the fact that its completed essence is incompletion. Yes, black's injunction is: "You who see me without seeing anything, go on!"

[7] Badiou is bringing out the conceptual connection here between Soulages' invented term *l'outrenoir* ("ultrablack" or "beyond black") and *l'outre-mer*, meaning "overseas" or "beyond the sea," which it clearly echoes.

Flags

There is no better way to test the symbolic consistency of a color than to examine how it appears on flags, and especially the point at which one color in particular takes over an entire flag.

The white flag, for example, accompanied the death throes of royalism for a while. As such, there's a "pastness," something melancholy, about it. It is to the flag what Chateaubriand is, not without distinction, to political literature: the last vestige of something that has no future. But in the final analysis the white flag is none-theless dishonored, and so is white, for being the universal symbol of surrender. To hoist the white flag is to surrender, to fail to say the word of Cambronne[8] when the enemy is pressing you to lay down your arms. At the very least, it is to evince a suspicious desire to negotiate in the heat of the battle. The formal rules of war, admittedly respected only with great difficulty, stipulate that persons waving a white flag are not to be fired upon. In this respect, the poor guys are comparable to ambulances.

More seriously perhaps, over the course of history the noncolor white itself, by contamination with its reactionary symbolic function, has changed into a negative symbol, no longer burdened by its "pure virgin"-type airs. Today, and for quite some time now, to say someone's a "white" is to say they're a reactionary, a counter-revolutionary, regardless of whether it was against the Blues during the Vendée War or against the Reds during the civil war in Russia. The whites, the blues, the reds . . . so what about the blacks? Well, the history of the black flag is once again very complicated.

[8] When asked by the English general Colvill to surrender at the Battle of Waterloo, the French general Cambronne is said to have boldly replied "*Merde!*" (which, in that context, meant something like "Go to hell!"). The euphemism *le mot de Cambronne* is used to this day.

Originally, let's face it, it was the flag of the sea pirates, and even today it's the flag of the desert pirates, the international, nomadic militia of the "Islamic State." Let's be very clear: whatever dubious admiration one might have for anything claiming to be independent of and opposed to civilized states, that particular black flag is explicitly nihilistic and deadly. As the sea pirates' flag, it featured, as everyone knows, a skull and crossbones. As the desert pirates' flag, it floats over the bloody celebrations of mass beheadings. Black, in this case, is only opposed to law-abiding lives to the extent that it is the emblem of a life dedicated to death. That black is a blood relation of the black surrounding the Prince of Darkness, the very one who declares in Goethe's *Faust*: "I am the one who always denies." However, while we must undoubtedly deny many things, it is solely on account of what we want to affirm. Thus, the nihilistic black of this kind of black flag is related to the Fascists' "*Viva la muerte*." Besides, weren't Mussolini's militiamen "Blackshirts"? And didn't Nazi officers love black uniforms? Wasn't the swastika on their flag a threatening black? Black's cause would seem to be lost here.

47

Except that the black flag is also the anarchists' flag. Black flags waved over revolutionary Barcelona right from the start of the Spanish Civil War; I myself saw them, the temporary companions of the exclusively red flags, in the big demonstrations of May '68 and its aftermath. The black flag is an always hard-to-control, often troublesome but always combative and ultimately necessary part of countless popular mass movements in every country in the world.

I will refuse to lump anarchists and fascists together here under the sign of black. To the model that's in fashion today – merging opposites, equating Stalin red with Hitler black and therefore, even more easily, anarchist black with fascist black – I will oppose instead the internal dialectic of black.

In the early philosophical stages of the Cultural Revolution, the Chinese communists stated that the essence of dialectics wasn't that "two combines into one" but that "one divides into two." This is completely the case with black: as a historical or political symbol, it has absolutely divided into two. Its rebellious vocation, its negative force, accounted for, and still accounts for, the nihilist subjectivity's barbaric acts, whenever "Satan calls the shots." But the other black, the black of anarchy, stood for a vision – albeit shallow or simplistic but nonetheless vibrant and fraternal – of hope in a reconciled world. There was nothing more characteristic in this regard than the split that occurred in 1879 in the Russian populist group Land and Liberty, which was engaged in the struggle against czarism on the basis of a newfound confidence in the people and in the peasant masses in particular. A dominant faction took the name "The People's Will," with attacks on despots becoming its major form of action. It was The People's Will that carried out the assassination of Alexander II in 1882. There is no doubt that, even though it was undeniably for a good cause, this faction shared many aspects of the nihilist subjectivity. The other faction was committed to patient, prolonged action among the people, in order to create a strong political organization among them. This was already the classic struggle between terrorist impatience and what Mao promoted as "prolonged work among the masses." Now, what name did this political faction choose for itself, in opposition to the nihilist-tinged anarchist impatience? "The Black Partition."

Black, as a symbol, is thus intrinsically divided, very broadly speaking, between impatient, murderous nihilism and a patience built on confidence in organization.

To be sure, the latter faction – I'll come back to this – ultimately aligned itself with red. But the fact that it could align itself with black implies a sort of strength in the dialectic that, symbolically, splits black apart.

What's more, a number of anarchist groups wave half-black, half-red banners. So let's say that when it comes to flags, there's the nihilist black-black and the communist red-black.

Red and black. And white. And violet.

I have spoken, and will speak again, about the so-called black vs. white opposition. But isn't it the opposition-tinged alliance between black and red that actually places black in a dialectical relationship with the real colors? Let's take a close look at this.

1. Catholic priests used to be dressed in black. They still are, in areas that haven't been swamped by modernity, which dissolves the priest in the vast sea of the consumer masses. This black was that of a sort of dress. It was a double paradox: the priest of the God of Consolation wore the colors of the Prince of Darkness, and, as the overseer of a strict hierarchical separation between the sexes, he dressed his hypothetical chastity as a woman.

Once again, we see the dialectics of black. Nietzsche, the greatest philosophical adversary of the priest, wanted to put an end to the deadly cult of the Crucified and sought in this way to "break the history of the world in two." The priest, for his part, breaks the history of black in two; he wrests it away from the Devil and makes it, as opposed to the virginal white that would be expected, the visible and feminized symbol of the service of faith and the abstinence it demands.

2. However, above the priest, high above, in the Roman lands of the Catholic monarchy, stands the cardinal. This hierarchical superior, the only one allowed to participate in the voting to elect the supreme leader (the Pope), is dressed in red: he wears – hopefully without pride, the ultimate sin – the "cardinalatial scarlet." It's as though black, often mocked by the masses (the priest as an asexual creep, in the form of a crow . . .), had to be surmounted with red when approaching the summits. Red would thus be the secret greatness of black. Or: God would see the immanence to black itself of its supposed opposite, the red blood of life, as that which elevates this black and brings it to its secret incandescence.

3. But at the very top, elevating the cardinalatial elevation of black by red, or of the priest at the base by the official of the summit, stands the Pope: in white! Thus, the priest divides black, the cardinal elevates it in red, and the Pope elevates this elevation in white, which is where it all comes to an end, since we thereby return to the age-old, false opposition between divisible black and indivisible white.

3a. Shall we say that, in between the base and the top, the bishop, who dresses in violet, lies in wait between the priesthood's lowly black and the cardinal's aristocratic red? The Church, in that case, would not be a rainbow. Cardinal red would be in the position of ultra-bishop violet, and at the very bottom end of the spectrum, priest black would take its revenge on its immediate superior, bishop violet, by observing that, in the light spectrum of the Church, bishop violet is merely an infra-cardinal red. Why not, after all? The Church by right stands above science. So let's bear its position in mind: the important colors are, in order, black, violet, red, and white. Yellow and blue will be left to be the colors of jesters' costumes, and salads will be left the dubious privilege of their mixture: green, which belongs to Nature, not God.

Stendhal: the red and the black

A famous novel by Stendhal also pairs red and black in its title. But the distribution is completely different. To be sure, the black seems to have become established as the black of the priest, since the Church was one of the options open to young Julien Sorel's existential ambition, and the most important servants of that ambition were, at least at the beginning, clergymen. But what about the red? There has been a lot of discussion about this. Was it the army? And specifically Napoleon, whose glory illuminates the young man's mind? But there was nothing particularly red about the army, after all, under either the Restoration or the Empire. The army, dressed in blue in the service of the despot, however much he may have been a "Robespierre on horseback,"[9] and then in the service of the nobiliary reaction, didn't look good in red.

Shouldn't we just cut straight to the crudest symbolism? The black: reaction in all its forms. The red: revolution in all its forms. And in Julien Sorel, the double drive of making a name for himself in society (the black drive) and of becoming detached (the red drive). A weak life drive and an overly strong death drive.

Aren't these the colors of the two women in his life? The shy, beautiful Madame de Rênal, the wife of a provincial mayor, is infatuated with her confessor, who will make her write the terrible letter of denunciation that leads to the tragedy and beheading of the hero at the end. The feisty Mathilde de la Mole reads Voltaire on the sly and gets them to give her her lover's decapitated head, which she kisses passionately, just as Salome did the head of Saint John the Baptist.

These women betoken a distinctive, colorful contrast: the black of clerical-bourgeois secrecy and treacherous denunciation versus the red of high-spirited youth and unrestrained passion.

[9] The phrase is Madame de Staël's.

Julien himself – and this is what makes him a character who we can say exemplifies the dialectics of black – is in many respects more elusive than sympathetic and more reckless than heroic. He embodies what I'd call all the shades of black, which, as I said, range not from white to black but from black-black to red-black: indeed, his life plays out in the divided darkness of his mind. The blood from his execution flows red, that's for sure, but it is with a sort of dark weariness that he has contrived and accepted such a fate.

Stendhal ultimately subtitled his book "A Chronicle of 1830." Ah, yes! The black of the Restoration lay between the red of the Revolution, which had already faded into the tricolor of the Empire, and the return of the red during the "Three Glorious Days" of 1830. In the midst of the black, Julien Sorel dreams of the red, or at the very least of the tricolor flag. In his own contradictory and deadly way he bears witness to that always crucial moment when it becomes clear that no blackness can hide forever the fact that its active essence is red, which is always, to a greater or lesser extent, the red of blood.

The dark desire of/for darkness

Yes, "Dark Desire" [Noir Désir] was the name of the most renowned French rock band, at the height of its fame in the 1990s and the early 2000s, torn to pieces by a single moment of murderous rage on the part of its leader, Bertrand Cantat, and later revived.[10] Who can forget the song "Tout disparaîtra mais / Le vent nous portera [Everything will disappear but / The wind will carry us]"?

The dark desire of/for darkness[11] . . . The same

[10] Convicted of involuntary manslaughter for murdering his actress girlfriend Marie Trintignant in 2003, Cantat spent four years behind bars, after which he rejoined the band until it broke up in 2010.

[11] The word *du* in the phrase *le noir désir du noir* can be translated as either "of" or "for," depending on the context. Here, owing to the essential ambiguity of the phrase, I have left both

song also evokes "That perfume of our dead years / What may come knocking at your door / Infinity of fates / You choose one and what do you retain of it? / The wind will carry it away."[12]

Spanning the centuries, this song is indeed the song of dark poetic desire, bound up with the melancholy of living, the song that whispered in the nascent French language 700 years ago:

What has become of my friends
Whom I held so close to me,
Whom I loved so much?
I believe they were planted too far apart,
They weren't sown well
And so they were lost.
Such friends did not treat me well,
Because while God was tormenting me
In so many ways
I did not see a single one in my house.
I believe the wind blew them away.

options open, as other translators have done, for example, with Lacan's well-known phrase "*le désir de l'autre*" (the desire of/for the other).

[12] The French line here, "*On en pose un et qu'est-ce qu'on en retient?*", plays on the words used in adding a sum in arithmetic: "Put down (a number) and carry (another number)."

Love is dead.
They are friends whom the wind blows away
And the wind blew hard in front of my door
Blew them away.[13]

Nor are black or white, or the couple they form, lacking in another melancholy lament, when Rutebeuf declares – under the telling title "The Demon of Winter": "In summer the black fly bites / And in winter, the white."

Indeed, the dialectic of black, in its poetic guise, seeks to include not just one of the aspects – either reactionary, *hence* nihilistic, or revolutionary *but* nihilistic – but the whole process that conjoins them in the existential meditation of a subject. That's why Cantat makes the wind play the game of a double evaporation: that of the "perfume of our dead years" and that of the decision to choose just *one* fate from among the infinity of those that may come knocking at the door of life. While Rutebeuf was already attempting to say that the black summer fly and the icy snow, that winter fly, were one and the same.

---

[13] "La Complainte de Rutebeuf" [Rutebeuf's Lament]. Rutebeuf's works were produced in the mid-thirteenth century.

The poem of dark desire is, in the end, that "black wind," come down to us from Dante, which makes the subject despair of being no more than someone circulating, throughout the dead years, in the assumed equivalence between black and white – or, at a deeper level, someone who, in our weariness of living, plots the betrayal of red-black by the forces of black-black.

Clothing

The black sign

In Western eroticism, black is the sign of the offering of an object: white nudity, like Mallarmé's "empty paper which its whiteness defends" against being marked up by poetry, is a whiteness undefended, or even offered up, only when marked with black. That's the very basics of artwork with claims to being erotic (or pornographic: it's the same thing): no body on its own is capable of what the same body decked out in black can do in the darkness of desire. Fishnet stockings and garter belts triumph eternally on the stage that makes a woman, gloriously, the object of every desire.

Nudity is essentially the already written text that desire needs only decipher by its action –

action that's always somewhat ludicrous and inferior to its object. As whiteness striated with black, as the palimpsest of its own glory, the body as such – evident substance, discontinuous opening, compelling discourse – seems to offer itself up to anyone who sees it, but also withdraws into the anonymous text that a woman becomes once she's become Woman.

Isn't it this black writing on flesh that's always assumed to be white (an assumption that is the flaw, or the moral fault, in this naïve fetishism, but I'll deal with this point down the line) that the censors' gray cloud tried to conceal, in the black-and-white photos of the smutty magazines of my youth? Because, back then, long before the time of disastrous hair removal, there was the conspicuous evidence of the often very luxuriant pubic tuft, which already marked the fatal location of femaleness. And even if in real life the tuft might have been blond, or even a flaming red, it was often black, not to mention that in the photos of the time everything blended together in the assumption of a dark triangle. It was this triangle that had to disappear at all costs.

But once again, the dialectic of black revealed its inexhaustible resourcefulness. For, with the same chaste gesture that, at the presumed location of what was not allowed to be seen, made the pubic darkness disappear into its white paper medium, the magazines endlessly displayed, on this same body supposedly free of its obscene darkness, underwear and accessories of the same black appearance: stockings, corsets, patent-leather heels, and other trinkets of desire loving to be deceived.

Thus, black always returns, one might say, all the more triumphant in that it only needed to shift a little bit, where desire is concerned, to defeat the whiteness that negates it.

Just as, by giving priority to women seen from the back in order to get around the censorship, the magazines turned obedience to the State into a cult of the position the priests called "*more bestarium*," or sodomy, so too, by displacing the black of the triangle onto the shoe or garter belt, they steadfastly encouraged fetishistic passion, whose aim, as has been known since Freud, is nothing less than to compensate for the lack on the female body that the naïve child thought he noticed there.

Black, in this way, consolidates one of its great affirmative functions: marking the location of what exists only by lacking.

Black humor, or black vs. black

Black is of course the color of mourning in our culture. I've mentioned everything associated with these infernal, deadly functions: black conceived of as absence of light, life extinguished, and primordial impurity. Indeed, behind the hearses draped with heavy black pall a crowd of mourners dressed in black slowly walks. And we assume that in their minds there is nothing but dark thoughts, meditation on the brevity of life and the inevitable death of everyone we love.

However, we also know that these dark thoughts are often the basis for healing jokes. Just think of all the funny stories we tell about disastrous funerals, the receptions that follow them, the inane small talk that helps pass the tedious time of the funeral service. All this is doubtless a kind of exorcism or defense against the ravages of the black-black that colors our mortal being.

What is this kind of humor called? Black humor! Black is once again on both sides of the existential fence, so to speak. As mourning, it makes us cry; as humor, it makes us laugh. And it will make us laugh about mourning itself.

At this juncture, the reader will not be spared a classic old joke:

It's the funeral of an old man. In the church hung with black are his wife, his sons, the whole family in mourning. The organ thunders, then the black-clad priest enters the pulpit to honor the deceased. He begins describing him: "Brethren, we are gathered today to mourn an admirable man. He was a devout Christian. He loved his children deeply. He was a good and faithful husband. He was the first to help his neighbor. He was courteous to a fault . . ."

On hearing all this, the widow, in a black dress, black hat, and black veil, has a nagging doubt. She whispers to her eldest son, who's seated beside her in a dark gray suit with a black armband: "Pierre, tiptoe up to the coffin and take a look inside. See whether it's really your father who's in it."

That's right! When black tries to make us laugh at blackness, our laughter may well be hollow.[14] Or our faces may turn gray.[15]

[14] There is an untranslatable pun here based on the French expression *rire jaune*. The last part of the line, translated literally, would read: "we may well laugh yellow."

[15] The expression Badiou uses here, *faire grise mine*, is usually translated as "to look morose," "to pull a long face," etc.

Outward appearance

This is the way things are.

In the service of death, the black of mourning is the extinction of all the lights of the human parade: all bodies are subject to the equality of that which, as the negation of light, prevents any one of them from shining more than the others. The dark equality before death.

In the service of sex, the black of the fetish illuminates, against an ostensibly white background, the object that desire carves out from the far too infinite, far too singular expanse of a subjectivated body. Here, black sees to it that the one woman becomes the One Woman, insofar as all women may do so. Dark repetition vis-à-vis sex.

Black circulates omnipotently, from the extinction of all singularity for lack of a human parade to its extinction from excess.

But what about black in everyday life? The black dress, the black jacket, the black shoes? The tailcoat, which turns every man into a penguin? The black hat?

The dialectic of black is not disrupted by any circumstances, whether ordinary or extraordinary. The "little black dress" forever remains a symbol of simple elegance, a sort of Idea of the dress, such that, stripped of all ostentation, subtle and suggestive, it nonetheless maintains – if it's a success, if it's "worn well" – a sort of miraculous exactness, while the tuxedo and its heavy-duty version, the aptly named "tailcoat," coolly remain, even under the sneers, proof of the fact that a rich bourgeois or the mayor of any city, when required to appear, can show up, wearing black marked with pure white, in the same stiff attire as a fallen prince. And it's even often in this black attire, as old-fashioned and uncomfortable as it is indestructible, that the man who is most bound by, most subjected to, a unique set of gestures, the man who is most responsible as much for ecstasy as for the possibility that there might not be any, appears before a large audience: the orchestra conductor.

Black worn this way testifies to its constitutive duality: it is a sign of simple elegance as well as a sign of the most ponderous, ostentatious complexity. Capable of freeing women from the oppressive, multicolored confections of the past. Capable of keeping men, for two centuries, in the formal yoke of starched collar and dragging black coattails.

It's true that the icy black sheen of the top hat has given up the ghost, proving Mallarmé's famous prophecy, which I'll remind you of, wrong: "given that it [the top hat] is, at a certain date in man's history, on heads, then it will always be there. Anyone who has put on such a thing can't take it off. The world would come to an end, but not the hat . . . "[16] Well, that hat seems to have reached the end of its line, yet the world goes on, more or less.

Nevertheless, the hat's sheen is found in identical fashion on formal dress shoes, those

[16] Stéphane Mallarmé, letter to Anatole La Vieillesse, in *Selected Letters of Stéphane Mallarmé*, ed. and tr. Rosemary Lloyd (Chicago: University of Chicago Press, 1988), 218.

expensive black masterpieces, shined to a high gloss. It's about these, rather than about the giant Rostabat defeated by Roland in *The Legend of the Ages* by Hugo (a very great master of black, Hugo was) that we should say: "And we saw the bottom of his black soles." At any rate, during formal ceremonies, black, having lost its head, takes comfort in still having its feet.

Physics, biology, and anthropology

The metaphorical black of the Cosmos

When you exclaim "I'm lost in the dark!" it no doubt has a first meaning: there's no light, you can't see a thing. But just as the word "light," and especially its plural, "lights" [i.e., the Enlightenment], came to mean, from the eighteenth century on, the triumph of science and rationalism, including revolutionary rationalism, so, too, "dark" has slipped from a purely visual connotation to a derived meaning, whose context is mental. The expression "I'm really in the dark" could then mean, for example, that you can't see how to continue the proof of a mathematical proposition you've been working on for days and nights on end.

Two essential metaphors of contemporary

cosmology must be attributed to a combination of the original and the derived meanings of the adjective *noir*: "dark matter" [*matière noire*] and "black hole" [*trou noir*].

The matter and the hole aren't "dark" or "black" in the exact same way.

It's the hole, for once, that possesses the fullness of meaning here. And it's even the hole, inasmuch as it is black, that denotes the most compact fullness! Let's take the easier case to describe: a star located near the center of the galaxy, having reached a certain stage of its evolution, implodes under the enormous attractive force of its predominantly iron core. Its outer layers disintegrate, generating a massive abyss of light, which is mistakenly called a "supernova": it was previously believed that a new star ("nova") was being created, but it was actually the *death* of the star. And its dark death, moreover, since, after a few spectacular weeks – its light can be equal to that of an entire galaxy – the star is reduced, as a result of this gravitational catastrophe, to its core alone. Inside the core, which from a cosmological perspective is minuscule, the particles are stuck to each other with no empty space at all between them. As a result, given its inconceivable density, it exerts such a tremendous attraction on everything that nothing – neither matter nor light – can escape from it. The star, in this at once shrunken and immensely powerful form, is therefore totally invisible. Even though existing, since no sign of this existence can be deduced from "what" exists, it makes a hole in all possible perception; it is a black hole in it.

But we should note: even though it's a hole in perception, and hence in relation to the presumed activity of a star detector in a galaxy, it is in no way a hole in the real. It is instead a kind of a magic sphere or ball: everything that comes near it immediately becomes part of it. As a negligible but mercilessly agglutinate mass, the dead star lies at the border between nothingness (the hole) and super-reality (a dense, self-contained mass that treats everything passing by it as indistinguishable from itself). As usual, black – very apt here for its misnomer "hole" – symbolizes, without distinction, both lack and excess.

Dark matter, unlike the misnomer "hole," is not the dark result of excessive light. It is certainly not the dark remnant of the implosion of a massive star, which might have lit up the immensity of the sky for a while, sometimes even in broad daylight. Instead, out of sight, it strives to fill a gap in thought. In a nutshell, if the matter of the universe were the matter that our scientific calculations measure of the "real" (everything observable or rationally deducible from observation), then galaxies, and to an even greater extent clusters of galaxies, wouldn't rotate the way we can see that they do. For these gigantic spirals of stars and their haphazard connections to rotate the way they do, there would have to be mass. A lot of mass, enormously more of it than we are able to "see". There would have to be at least six or seven times more!

As usual, we black out whatever we don't know. We hypothesize that an astronomical (so to speak) quantity of "dark matter" exists. The details are far from being finalized, and theories as complex as they are contradictory compete with one another . . . But the fact remains that "dark" in this way *designates what is lacking in perception so that nothing should be lacking in thought.*

Thus is confirmed that the black of the Cosmos is not so much the black of night, that poetic opposite of the blue of the sky, as it is the name for what has disappeared (the black hole), the name for any possible perception as well as for everything that ought to exist (dark matter) so that there should be nothing lacking in the concept. In the end, what the black of the Cosmos connotes is less absence or death than what thought opposes to them.

One additional note: in that universal glue of empiricism, the English language, this dialectic of black is accepted only grudgingly. Lack and excess? Perception versus concept? "*Shocking Platonism!*"[17] So English-speaking empiricists don't say "black matter," they say "dark matter," hence *matière sombre*. "Come on," they say, "it's not nothingness, it's not pure concept! It's just matter that's still too dimly illuminated. Someday, it will be light. And we will see."

[17] In English in the text.

The secret blackness of plants

From what we can see of it, the plant world has hardly any black in it. Rather, on a stunning background where every shade of green is explored, the plant world is, for our dazzled eyes, the apotheosis of colors. All over the world, flowers are the beautiful symbol of true color, whose different shades we artfully cultivate, while we explore roses' infinite gamut of fragrances, tulips' erectness, cattleya orchids' refined rarity, and chrysanthemums'[18] gift to the poor dead who, "hidden in earth where they / Are warmed and

[18] Chrysanthemums are associated with death in French culture and are typically placed on graves on All Saints' Day, November 1.

have their mysteries burnt away,"[19] suddenly feel much better, almost alive.

The plant world rises as, apart from it, only deserts and high mountains do, to the spatial challenge of the oceans, their measurelessness. It has become – it deserved better, perhaps, than this ambiguous pedigree – the banner of contemporary political environmentalism. In democratic assemblies everywhere now, seats are proudly held by Green Party members, who no doubt think, because of this, that they're on intimate terms with nature's abundance. In any case, there is no worse insult for a Green than to be called black – naturally not in the sense of Africans but in that of Mussolini's followers' shirts.

Should we conclude that plants are the symbol of nonblack, of the dethroning of black by the brilliance of the colors on the green felt of the world's gaming table? This would seem to be implied by Alexandre Dumas' having made the "black tulip," in a famous novel of his, into the

---

[19] Paul Valéry, "The Graveyard by the Sea," tr. C. D. Lewis in *The Complete Poems of C. D. Lewis* (Stanford, CA: Stanford University Press, 1996), 410.

symbol of the impossible, the ultimate flower, the paradoxical Idea of the flower, the Platonic Flower, in short, which all the main characters, in a historically complicated Holland, compete to develop.

And yet, and yet . . . The black radish alone should make us suspicious!

For it may well be – as the radish attests – that the true essence of flowers, and stems, and branches, and leaves, is what tethers them to Mother Earth, that immense system for capturing water, sap, beneficial bacteria, and mushrooms maintained in a productive parasitic alliance – in a nutshell, the subterranean blackness of roots.

What would that enormous tree, that hive of bee-leaves, that solar buzzing high above our heads, be if it hadn't grown one day from a rotten fruit fallen on the ground, and if, at every stage of its growth, it hadn't secured its foundation through a tangled underground web as big as itself, and far stronger, gnarly, and riddled with rootlets? On the invisible underside of the green ground and its panoply of colors lies the black network of roots, of which the black radish is just one tiny witness.

This is what Hugo understood, guided as he

was by the sure instinct that made him see everywhere the hidden blackness all life requires and
produces, just as he recreated the slimy depths of
the sewers underneath Paris-the-City-of-Lights.
In the poem "The Satyr" he showed this symbol
of natural life, this secret enemy of the light of
the gods, in its deep, so to speak, relationship
with the plant world. He probed its subterranean
reality. Unlike superficial painters, who are
endlessly inspired by bouquets and bushes, and
unlike elegiac poems, which are nothing but
glosses on roses, the satyr goes straight to the
heart of things:

> *The satyr seemed lost in the vast abyss;*
> *He gave a root's-eye view of trees; depicted*
> *Murderous plants in subterranean combat –*
> *Caverns unknown to light, but known to fire –*
> *The shadowy underside of the creation.*[20]

Here we go! The essential, secret blackness of
plants only reveals itself to those who, far from the

[20] Victor Hugo, "The Satyr," in *A Bilingual Edition of the
Major Epics of Victor Hugo*, vol. 1, ed. and tr. E. H. Blackmore
and A. M. Blackmore (Lewiston, NY: The Edwin Mellen Press,
2002), 313.

Greens' fantasies, understand the subterranean vegetal frenzy, the murder below ground, the vegetal black hole into which no light can enter. And to do so you have to be able to depict "the root's-eye view of trees," which, rather than to some childish idolizing of Mother Nature, of the goddess Gaia, leads you straight to "the shadowy underside of the creation," to the blackness of which nature's greenery is both the product and the mask.

And so Hugo was able to understand that the plant world, subject to its secret blackness and hardened by the "subterranean combat" of "murderous plants," is not a symbol of peace and harmony but, on the contrary, the quintessence of all predation and devouring. Forget about garden parties and picnics in the woods. Let's see what the satyr's eye enables us to understand. Let's see what plants, true to their birth and their ongoing support in the black of the earth, are:

> *. . . consuming*
> *Rain and consuming wind; night or death, all things*
> *To them are good; corruption sees the roses*
> *And brings them nourishment; voracious grasses*
> *Browse in the wooded depths; things can be heard*

Crunching between plants' teeth, at every time;
And the rustic Immensity, far off,
On every side, can be seen pasturing;
Trees, in their mighty progress, transform everything;
Grit, sand, and clay, are needed – needed by
Lentiscus, yews, and brambles; and the earth
Watches with joy the terrible forest eating.[21]

Is that the last word, though? Do we have to give up the floral charm of colors? No, Hugo himself would say. Here, too, black is divisible: what the plant world's devouring produces, against a backdrop of subterranean blackness, is ultimately also the flowers of shimmering life and constant, comforting color. And so, to the darkness of human death nature opposes the everlasting life that a flower in the wind, all by itself, signifies. Consider, once again, in the poem "Words on the Dune," the splendid dramatization of the dialectic between black in its negative human version – death and sorrow – and the as it were eternal blue of which every plant's hidden blackness is capable:

[21] Ibid., 313.

Oh how our memories are neighbors of remorse!
How everything makes us weep more!
Oh, how cold I feel touching you, oh death,
Black bolt on humanity's door!

So I dream, listening to winds groan and roar
And waves wrinkle toward the land.
Summer is laughing, and you can see, on the shore,
Blue thistle blooming in the sand.[22]

I should point out, in conclusion, that, while in symbols and flags it is red that elevates black, often in art – and this can be seen in Soulages' marvelous black/blue paintings as well as in this poem – it is blue's task to establish the positive reverse side of black. No doubt also because the sky, our universal roof, forever alternates, or at least so it seems to us, between the blue of day and the black of night.

[22] *Victor Hugo: Selected Poetry*, tr. Steven Monte (Manchester: Carcanet Press, 2001), 161.

Animal black

There is no doubt that there are black animals. True, it's a question of fur, or shells. Rarely, if ever, and I'll come back to this, is it a question of black skin. But animals' hair can be black, and this is the case with the human species, too. No one would deny that there is jet-black hair associated with different hair-covered areas on the body. It's just that many animals, unlike the human species, have more than just a sort of skullcap, a shadow around their genitals, tufts of hair under their arms, or even a few blackish streaks on their chest or thighs. These animals are completely covered in black hair: panthers and horses, for the most part, cats somewhat less so, and dogs somewhere in between. Or in black feathers: crows have long had the contradictory reputation typical of their color. They were thought to be sinister creatures and bad omens, but also to be the familiars of seers, the trusty predictors of the future. If a crow flies by on your left, watch out! But if it flies by on your right, you can breathe easy! The crow symbolizes the flight of black toward its opposing destinations. The deep black and pure white of Normandy cows already smells of milk. And let's not forget the penguin! Black and white, it waddles over the ice like some bewildered orchestra conductor.

There are also the masses of beetles with their brilliant, shiny black shells. Busy ground beetles and patient dung beetles alike make black glisten, even in the dirt. Many weevils (insects whose incredible numbers are frightening: there are probably more than 200,000 different species in the world) are a somewhat drab, striated black, as though to hide under this unassuming shell the extreme damage they inflict as crop pests.

In the oceans there's the black of dolphins, sharks, and whales, not to mention the dark gray of seals. So it's as if black helps them slip into the bitter cold water without being affected by it. Black is the sleek, featureless protective covering of those living submarines: when they dive, there's no drama, just pure gracefulness; the black swish of the tail is silent . . . The black swimmer glides around like an ominous shadow. And that's why even humanoid divers' rubberized wetsuits are black: so that they might be mistaken for sharks, albeit somewhat ungainly ones.

Almost everywhere in the animal kingdom black has to confront colors, very bright ones because they aren't the living skin but the fur, the feathers, the shells, the active surface, the sexual ornamentation. There can be cats with three colors: red and white border whimsically on black. The pseudo-dialectic of black and white is a widespread affectation, from colts to rabbits. And the zebra takes it to extremes by distributing its black stripes according to a scheme that differs for each animal: so many zebras, alive and dead, so many marvelous, distinct abstract paintings. Among birds and fish the symphony is brilliant: the reds, yellows, blues, and greens punctuate the black in the flapping wings of the bird taking flight and in the glint of the fish's leap on the waves. Insects bring to perfection the aristocratic association of black velvet and gilt: they make black drops of light shimmer on butterflies' wings!

All in all, animal black is a peaceful black, at once ubiquitous and tolerant. Life in general, or nature, has no bone to pick with black, whether it be coal, beetle, dog, or whale. Or the dark night into which the days all sink, the night of crime, no doubt, of predators and their victims, but also the night of mating, whereby all living things persist in living.

It is man and man alone who changed the black of the crow, or of the cat, into something evil. It is man who opened the case against black.

An invention of white people

We should definitely begin with a famous question of Jean Genet's in the preface to his play *The Blacks*: "What is a Black? And first of all, what color is he?"

Indeed. After demonizing black cats, the Devil's dark powers, crows, witches in black rags, the darkness of death, and the blackness of the soul, we so-called Whites of Western Europe had to invent the fact that the majority of Africa's inhabitants clearly constituted an inferior "race," condemned to slavery and then to the forced labor of colonial occupation simply because this enormous population was "black." Solely on the basis of this so-called color, millions of human beings were transported like cattle to the other side of the ocean and chained in ships' holds, with the result that a very large number of them died during the passage. The survivors were sold to rich landowners and worked for them under conditions that were absolutely comparable to those of ancient slavery. Large French cities like Bordeaux and Nantes, which specialized in this traffic, owed their prosperity to it. In 1885, well after the superficial "abolition of slavery," a politician like Jules Ferry, who is still revered by the "left" today, publicly stated: "I repeat that superior races have a right, because they have a duty. They have the duty to civilize inferior races . . . "[23] They "civilized" them all right, with lashes of the bullwhip on the plantations.

For the vast majority of colonized Africans, the most benign solution, available to only a scant minority of them, was to become a servant of the colonists. Every colonist had his "boy," which is only logical, isn't it? A civilizer deserves to be well served. Even today, countless Africans risk their lives trying to make it to Europe. To do what

[23] Jules Ferry, *Speech before the French National Assembly, 1883.* Cited in *Modern Imperialism: Western Overseas Expansion and Its Aftermath,* ed. Ralph A. Austen (Lexington, MA: Heath, 1969), 71.

there? To be construction workers or dishwashers in restaurants, where the men are concerned, or cleaning ladies or nannies, where the women are concerned. That's right! Either you're "inferior" – because you're black – or you're not.

In the United States, the so-called democracy that still controls the West, black slavery had become so huge a phenomenon (there were more than three million slaves in 1860) that it took a bloody civil war and more than 800,000 dead, in the middle of the nineteenth century, to achieve its legal abolition. And this abolition allowed such strong discrimination in every domain and such deeply ingrained underlying racism to persist that, today, the "black question" remains a sort of unhealable wound in American society, even though the President is "black." This is how "black," precisely during the economic and military triumph of the "Whites," became a despised epithet, an ineradicable stigma, for humanity.

This set-up, rooted in a phantasmatics of colors, was – and still is – so powerful, and it proved to be so effective as an immoral justification of the worst evil, that the Europeans and their colonialist offspring the world over undertook a hierarchical color-coding of all of humanity. At the top there was the white race, that of the colonial conquerors. Then came the Yellows, who were very inferior, of course, but more complicated, "inscrutable," tenacious, and difficult to control. Next came the Redskins, who had been exterminated for the most part by the Yankee colonists, so forget about them. And finally there were the Blacks, the negroes, all the way at the bottom. When I was a child I used to consult an illustrated Larousse encyclopedia that dated from the 1930s, from only yesterday, in short. It contained an article accompanied by definitive illustrations "proving" that a black man's skull was halfway between an ape's and a white man's.

A milestone in this whole business is surely the aptly named Black Code, drawn up by the royal administration in France in the seventeenth century to regulate slavery in France's Caribbean possessions. Contrary to what is sometimes said, this code, which was of course a pro-slavery abomination, was nevertheless ahead, so to speak, of the republican Larousse of the 1930s. It validated slavery and its hereditary nature. But it criticized what it called the "prejudice of color,"

94

namely, the theory of black people's inherent inferiority. It said that once a black person was freed, he or she had the same rights as a white person. So it is clear that modern colonial racism, which is anti-slavery in principle, replaced an abhorrent form of social relations validated by color (a person, by virtue of being black, could be bought and thus become the property of someone else) by biologized social relations, racism, which to my mind is even more abhorrent (a person, by virtue of being black, is inherently, and not merely owing to his or her social status, inferior to a white person).

The revolt against the hierarchical stigmatization of part of humanity on account of its so-called color – black, in this case – can take two different forms.

The first consists in confirming the role of colors. It will be said that part of humanity is indeed black, but the hierarchy of values will be eliminated, or even reversed: blacks are strictly equal to whites, or anyone else, or even: blacks are more attractive, stronger, smarter, more in tune with nature, sexier, have more rhythm, are more graceful, more ancient, have a more complex symbolic order, are more poetic, more this or more that, than whites. In a nutshell: "Black is beautiful."

The second consists in denying that color has any relationship whatsoever with any system of valorization or disparagement. This means that any overall judgment, whether positive or negative, of a supposed "community" of color is rationally impossible. Color is of course an objective determination, but it must have no symbolic extension.

I can suggest a more radical version of the second approach. Naturally, I accept its universalist consequences, but I go further: there is not even any objectivity to the judgment of color. In reality, no color can be assigned to a given human being, not black, of course, but not white or yellow or any color identity whatsoever either. An individual can be predicated as black and classified in the "Black people" category only through the use of a very rough and pointless approximation.

The first approach, in its most radical form, had its poets and singers, particularly between 1930 and 1980 or thereabouts. The poets sang of what was then called "negritude," or the positive assertion of blackness, which was considered the soul of both African humanity and the portion of it that had been deported to America. Basically, they sang of black people's greatness.

Everyone, alas, has heard about the defects, ignorance, backwardness – the barbarism, in short – that white people still have the unmitigated gall to ascribe to the so-called "black" Africans. Only a short time ago Sarkozy, that ignorant little guy, had the audacity to lecture the Africans, from the heights of his undiminished colonialist paternalism, and tell them that they've remained "on the margins of History"! Well, all these "obvious facts" that whites have been spouting for several hundred years about so-called blacks, all these clichés, were adopted by the negritude movement – without even bothering to discuss them or separate fact from fiction – as the basis for establishing black people's unconditional, indeed exemplary, belonging to the past and present history of humanity. That superlative poet, Aimé Césaire, gave this vision its most intense expression:

My negritude is not a stone, its deafness hurled against
    the clamor of the day
my negritude is not a leukoma of dead liquid over the
    earth's dead eye
my negritude is neither tower nor cathedral

it takes root in the red flesh of the soil
it takes root in the ardent flesh of the sky
it breaks through opaque prostration with its upright
   patience.[24]

It is the "upright patience" here that makes blacks, as negritude would have it, the most essential earthly witnesses of what it means to belong to humanity. But for others, especially in the United States, it was, on the contrary, the most extreme impatience, the hunger for immediate action and its splendid fury, that were and still are acclaimed as the means by which blacks can stand beyond the categories of the imperious West. The movements of that era were called, for example, "the Black Panther Party," a name that was directly inscribed in the dialectics of black: the black panther is the epitome of animal beauty, but it is also the fiercest, most graceful of felines, the one that prowls by night as a terrifying, unconscious menace in white people's dull dreams. Thus, blacks, vis-à-vis whites, assume

[24] Aimé Césaire, *Notebook of a Return to the Native Land,* ed. Annette Smith and tr. Clayton Eshleman (Middletown, CT: Wesleyan University Press, 2001), 35.

total pride in their blackness and can lay claim to their natural superiority.

It is easy to understand these approaches: since the whites have called us blacks, why shouldn't we turn this name against their power? The dialectic of colors is very dense here. Black, a stigmatizing category internal to white domination, is reappropriated by its victims as the banner of their revolt. The blacks are thus between two whites: the whites who invented the blacks in order to enslave and segregate them, and the whites who are the target of the blacks' insurgent independence.

These are irreversible gains of the 1960s and 1970s: those red years also reinvented the black revolutionary, who had already, in the orbit of the Revolution of 1789, created his glorious and quasi-definitive figure in the guise of Toussaint Louverture. This was the case, as we've just seen, in the United States, and it was also the case in Africa, where a whole generation of revolutionary leaders were able to speak about the conditions of real freedom to their subjugated peoples: Nkrumah, Lumumba, Um Nyobé, Amilcar Cabral, and so on. All of them were also either assassinated or overthrown by the colonial powers' secret services, the armies of intervention, or the puppet leaders' mercenaries. Nevertheless, from Toussaint Louverture to them, you could learn that "black" in any case didn't mean slavery, servitude, or collaboration.

There is no doubt that we must go beyond this now. Or, rather, go elsewhere. Already, in fact, in political action, and notwithstanding the phrase "black power," the dominant vision of militant American blacks, like that of Toussaint Louverture and the revolutionary leaders in Africa, wasn't segregationist. It included, to be sure, the temporary need for an independent black organization, with no whites in it. But that was just to mark the rupture, to root out the remnants of a submissive mentality in black people, and to get them used to the tasks of leadership and thought required by the revolutionary enterprise. What's more, united action with majority "white" organizations was the rule for the most part. Thus, the most radical "white" organization, the Weathermen, lent a helping hand from time to time to the Black Panthers. The gradual dissolution of the whole black–white dialectic was already underway in favor of political universalism, even if that process might be a long one and include a significant period of time during which the blacks would retake possession of their capacity to exist on their own terms and no longer have to imitate the forms and rituals of white domination.

In sum, the first revolutionary approach, proud negritude, prepared the ground for the second, namely that, while there are of course different communities, and the black community in particular, they must all have strictly the same rights. In the final analysis, equality must also be the equality of colors. This is a specifically American concern: society is a patchwork of communities – racial, sexual, differently colored, professional, ethnic, and so on. And the best that can be hoped for is that all these communities coexist peacefully and have the same rights. Thus, the political question ended up being a legal question. The equality of action and creation, so vibrant in the 1960s and 1970s, hardened into law, under the auspices of a so-called benevolent State. And colors, under the heading of "cultural differences," remain as the focus of paternalistic attention in academic postcolonial studies.

I think we need to take one step more and adopt the "hard" version of the second approach.

The maxim would then become: to put an end to any use of so-called colors in all forms of deliberation and collective action. We need to establish once and for all that a politics of emancipation has nothing to do with colors – in terms of norms and hierarchies, of course, but also in terms of objectivity.

To Genet's question "What color is a Black?" we must answer that, as far as humanity as a whole is concerned, there are actually no colors. And not a white's any more than a black's.

Try to *really* decide what someone's color is. Is a white person white? Certainly not! The only white person I know of is the white clown, with his powdered head, the image of a somewhat stupid kind of common sense as compared with his sidekick Auguste, whose main feature is a big red nose. In fact, passing through an endless number of gradations of skin tone, we call someone who's paler than a supposedly black person "white." We thus go from certain Swedes, let's say, to certain Mauritanians, by way of many Asians. Some Tamils are moreover much darker than many "black" Africans, without their being put in the "Black" category. Many Africans are dark-skinned without our being able to say they're black, many Europeans are much too dark for it to be reasonable to say they're white, some Asians, who are anything but yellow (besides, who's yellow? Someone suffering from hepatitis, perhaps?), are often lighter-skinned than many southern Europeans, and the blackest of men, if compared with a black dye or even a lump of coal, instantly stops being visible as black.

Truth be told, the distinctive feature of human beings is doubtless to be more or less dark-skinned, with an infinite gradation of shades, but actually not to be any one specific color. And why is this so? Because people are not covered with fur or feathers or a chitinous shell. They are the only animals who are naturally naked, and their skin only has a variety of shades and no fixed color.

This is the most striking difference, in terms of pure visibility, between the human animal and the apes. Seen from a distance, a gorilla sitting and playing with a stick can look incredibly like us on account of his posture and gestures. But he is *really* black, because his fur, which covers his body from head to toe, is black. Likewise, an orangutan looks like an old man, except that he's completely covered in red fur.

The clearest objective feature of the human

animal is that it doesn't have any color. And in particular it's impossible for it to be black, really black, any more than it can be white, let alone yellow or red (except in the case of severe sunburn).

Let's say that human beings go in an unbroken line from a somewhat mottled ultra-white light appearance to an infra-black dark appearance, and no classification is a match for the untold infinity of these skin tones.

Blacks, Yellows, Reds, and especially Whites were nothing but false "objective" bases for oppressive classifications, dubious symbolic calculations, disparaging judgments, or shameful displays of self-satisfaction.

So we need to beware of any symbolization, collective assessment, political venture, or overall judgment that would purport to include a color, of any kind, in its system.

In the universal order to which humanity aspires, neither white nor black has the slightest right to exist. *Humanity, as such, is colorless.*